BLESSINGS FOR THE HANDS

PHOENIX POETS

MATTHEW SCHWARTZ

Blessings for the Hands

THE UNIVERSITY OF CHICAGO PRESS
Chicago and London

MATTHEW SCHWARTZ is a writer and editor living in
Brooklyn, New York.

The University of Chicago Press, Chicago 60637
The University of Chicago Press, Ltd., London
© 2008 by The University of Chicago
All rights reserved. Published 2008
Printed in the United States of America

17 16 15 14 13 12 11 10 09 08   1 2 3 4 5

ISBN-13: 978-0-226-74094-2 (cloth)
ISBN-13: 978-0-226-74095-9 (paper)
ISBN-10: 0-226-74094-3 (cloth)
ISBN-10: 0-226-74095-1 (paper)

Library of Congress Cataloging-in-Publication Data
Schwartz, Matthew, 1977–
    Blessings for the hands / Matthew Schwartz.
        p. cm. — (Phoenix poets)
    ISBN-13: 978-0-226-74094-2 (alk. paper)
    ISBN-10: 0-226-74094-3 (alk. paper)
    ISBN-13: 978-0-226-74095-9 (pbk. : alk. paper)
    ISBN-10: 0-226-74095-1 (pbk. : alk. paper)
    I. Title.
    PS3619.C4875B55 2008
    811'.6—dc22

                                          2007025655

Contents

III

Acknowledgments

Grateful acknowledgment is made to the editor of *Alaska Quarterly Review* in which "Greeting," "Minor Parts," "Visitors," and "Photograph, for a Class on Perspective" first appeared.

I'd like to acknowledge the guidance, love, and support that have come from so many people in the course of writing this book. I owe a great deal to the writing community at the University of California, Irvine, which has supported my work in countless ways. Thank you to the many writers there who read early drafts of these poems. Thank you to Jim McMichael and Michael Ryan, who have been enduring examples to me of passionate intelligence. Working with them has deepened my life and work immeasurably, and deepened my sense that a life in poetry can be lived as a calling, a vocation. Their caring faith in my work is something for which I'll always be grateful. Thank you also to Martha Rhodes for her endless energy and support. She helped me break many habitual patterns in these poems, and always reminds me to push my writing into more daring, intimate places.

Several teachers at Sarah Lawrence College gave me the first sense I had of what mature poems are, and what it might mean to devote one's self to writing poetry. Their influence is present in these pages, and I'd like to acknowledge them here. Thank you to Michael Klein for his encouragement and enthusiasm. Thank you to Suzanne Gardinier for her clear-eyed compassion, her loving spirit, her wonderful sense of what a poem (and poetry itself) can be, and her laughter. Thank you to Victoria Redel for challenging my work as it grew, whose voice I still hear when I'm searching for the right word. Thank you to Kevin Pilkington for his support and his unerring sense of what is essential in a poem.

For various suggestions and sustaining encouragement, thank you to Ann Lauinger, Jaimee Kuperman, Marka Knight, Gary Atwood, and Maya Katz.

Thank you to UC Irvine for the 2002 Fletcher Jones Fellowship. Thank you to UC Irvine and the International Institute of Modern Letters for the 2003 Glenn Schaeffer Award. I'm forever grateful for the time they gave me to work on this project.

Thank you to my family, who has given me so much love and courage, especially my mother and sister, who inform so many of these poems so deeply. In many ways, this book is written for them.

And thank you to the folks at the University of Chicago Press for their support, especially Randy Petilos.

Greeting

She's a stranger, and for several days, when we pass, she smiles at me
and says "bless you, child, bless you."

It's so startlingly unexpected and pure that I almost flinch.
She must see something in my crutches, in the way I walk,
the injury of a relative, of herself,

but eventually I almost get used to it, the way she stretches out
the word "child," the way I bless her too, laughing.

How we started talking about her education, I don't remember,
but when she mentions Catholic school, I remember my mother's stories,
Sister Grace breaking the skin on her knuckles with a ruler,
and how happy I was that she could joke about it.

So there was a classroom and a room for punishment, my friend says,
and a coat closet next to that room, and the punished boy once
snuck into the closet and zipped twenty winter coats together,
dragged the whole thing down the hall—no one heard him—

and when the class came to see his suffering, everyone saw
how he marched out smiling, saw the splayed arms and collars and hoods
he wrapped around himself like a cape.

Even the teachers laughed, she said, even the teachers.

What did they think he did wrong?
What did they think he was supposed to learn?
What did it sound like, the stunned laughter of the teachers?
What did it look like, that coat, that punishment coat, that lop-sided, secretly
assembled coat?

Bright Drink

The waiter asked me
Why do you hold on to eternity so long?

handed me a two hundred dollar drink
sparkling in a thin glass,

appetite's brightness
that I held back from the world and fed, afraid,

wanting a world of appetite
to dull it, distill it, starve it.

I practiced grief like money.

The years I took to call it fear
not gone now, but more particular.

Yes, particular thirst attends me.
Yes, there is a voice

under outrageous debt
that brings me a bright drink asking why.

Minor Parts

I flailed above a wide wooden stage,
hanging from Saturn's wobbly rings.

Down there, I was the enchanter
with a yarn beard, in a dragon kimono.
I was the fat friar cracking jokes.

I was the chorus voice, the inner voice, the whisper, the spell,
playful and strangely anonymous.

I couldn't claw a grip, and shut my eyes
to get at the real Saturn, any gravity it had
to catch me, but I had to let go

and instead of hitting the stage, I kept falling.
I wanted anonymous weight to hold me there.

I wanted words I could spin with like the planets
leaking back out into the spinning
inarticulate world, but then,

the floor I fell through was the world I knew.
I wanted my body to surprise me by being there.

Necessity

In one greedy drag I had the whole cigarette in my throat,

my friend who always smoked watching me in our old living room.

He laughs nervously and points at me, at how my lungs are wrong,

at every ugly fear I want to talk out of but stutter to keep,

every breathed-in lived-in excess I need to shed like a husk because nothing

needs me but my fear, and when he steps outside the door and fans the stink away

I shout no you can't just wave it out like that—it's in the carpet and the walls

and our nails and minds and everything else that's not really here

and you have to point at every inch of spit and poison, every filter,

every history that can kill you, and taste it, every flinch that craves

the fury of no no no, every myth of punishment you're belly to belly with

saying no. Squint and see it. Nothing hunched in the thick room can claim me.

I'll run further out, through my throat's diaspora to my loosened

mouthful of coward stars, looking down at me as I am now,

faithful and unafraid.

Hannah

My sister, just born,
stubborn-gummed,
gnawed at my breast, expecting
milk. When she cried
she couldn't yet put
her whole body
behind her voice, or her voice was
not ready for her body
and seemed to come to her mouth
and me from a distance.
I laughed and rocked her,
careful not to laugh too loud.
Not a fat rolling laugh,
but not remote, not as her body
seemed then to her voice.

After Dinner, Laughing

I left for the other coast,
you for California.

Your voice was in both of us,
calling the known life falseness,

heavy as fact:
I don't know what I was waiting for.
You wanted to leave, so you left.

After years of not seeing each other,
we became our laughter—
stranger, farther from ourselves.

for Andrew Allan

Obligation

My mother's boyfriend, divorced like her, just as heavy with need,
would come home from always falling behind
and work his hands in the garden till they ached.

Whatever was in front of him consumed him—
juicing bags of grapefruit, watching the hockey game,
asking how my day was. His caring was overly serious,

as if repenting for whatever my mother, or I, or he,
never knew about his first marriage, or why he stayed
in it so long. I knew he was more generous than he

needed to be with his ex-wife and kids, and that they
always wanted more. We tried to help him talk about
all the mistakes he found on the construction site.

Try to forget it, for now, we'd say, you've done enough.
What would you do if you didn't have to work?
Where would you go, if you could?

He never remembered his dreams, even when we asked him.
My mother dreamt of a roller coaster ride with my father,
and told him how the screaming reassured her.

That's interesting, he said, and sounded like he meant it.
After dinner, we'd stay outside to watch the city's
moving lights. It was strange to say nothing, but I needed

to see him this way—and maybe he needed to see me—
grieving, wanting to look past the grief in labor, or generosity.

Division

My sister saw the top five floors of a high-rise
on fire, on the six o' clock news,
and thought it could be our house.

She called it "the fire thing,"
and couldn't sleep for a week.
Her shadow, closet, bed, body,

the fire thing, the fire thing.
She'd even sleepwalk
to the living room, a wild,

lost look on her face,
find my lap like a reflex,
then wander to bed again.

The next night, I said: pretend you are
a speck of dust, a cotton ball, a trampled flower,
something helpless in wind

that gets caught in wind
and travels over rooftops and storm clouds,
and comes back to the same bed.

Here is the rug, the rocking chair.
Here is the moon, the lampshade.
See them leaving their places?

The story's already leaving us,
running where we'd least expect.
Your body will come back to you

changed in your sleep,
back from its animal and spirit flights,
remembering.

After how long? It never matters.
Change is a secret there for both of us.
For you, waiting in school

with long division, remainders, numbers unresolved.

Visitors

They'd float in overcoats
through cobblestone streets,
or peek from magazines,
or glide through the grocery store.

That smoothness shined in the skin, the spindly
blue-gray bodies—the face,
that curious hint of a grin,

black sideways teardrop eyes
that could have contained
all of me, of them, the street, the world.

It was terrible at first, how they slipped
into the otherness of ordinary things,
and waited in my waking distances.

What comes back to me now is the stillness
in the eyes, how complete it is.

If I keep my thoughts that still,
will I find myself somewhere in the sky, light-years away?

Maybe the sky is a thought that takes years to form.
Maybe that's what terror is: a stillness wholly other, wholly mine.
Maybe I move like thought in many worlds.

Bodyweight

My crutches felt heavier than I was.
They landed with a thick thud on the blacktop
each time I took a step. I had to watch how I walked

so I didn't fall, like the other kids expected.
I liked to leave my crutches half-buried
behind the sandbox, where I couldn't see them,

and creep up the uneven monkey bars
arced like the upper half of a globe.
I wanted to see the whole playground.

The rungs crowded too close together,
and none of them was shaped the same.
I lifted my feet slowly to keep my braces quiet

against the metal. At the top, I could still hear
the jump rope flying, my friend throwing
handfuls of sand. I slipped. I locked my arms

tighter around whatever bars I could reach, and my leg
tensed and shook and hit the rung too close to me
when I tried going down, and my foot shot

through the gap, and dangled there.
I thought I could maybe slide out.
I thought my body could fit like my foot did,

but I was stuck. Everyone could see me,
everyone could hear me asking myself
What do I do with my body if it's

not a secret?

Generations

1.
Every Passover, my grandfather couldn't wait to eat,
and his lips looked braced against imagined pain.

His sister-in-law, at least, could smile, could talk
about work, and the subway, and going out with her neighbor.

I saw shoulders through the cabinets.
Clara and Grandma, crying over the soup.

Later, we would talk about suffering,
and what the food meant.

Clara sat quietly through most of the night,
being punished for her smile.

2.

After my grandparents died,
we cleaned the rows of music boxes
in the room behind the kitchen.

Clara tried to hum one of the songs.
We could barely hear the notes
over the gears churning.

My mother asked about whatever photo
she flipped to in the stacked albums,
and Clara tried to keep up:

where they were born,
what they did for a living,
when they died.

Stuck between two pages,
a photo with the border coming apart
falls out: Clara, in her twenties,
with fuller lips, in a white dress.

Beautiful, Beautiful we say, and she
turns away to tell us more
about anyone we don't know.

3.
Clara forgets what my voice sounds like on the phone,
where I live, what my mother is up to.

Her voice nestles and settles in her shelves
filled with the old house: a busted camera,

the pounds of coins we'd found in a cabinet,
the dates worn thin, the same few faces

blurring at the cheekbones, the hairlines.
When I touch any corner the whole frame shivers.

The porcelain ballerina next to my school pictures
gasps its lullaby through fifty years.

Poem for Maya

Who told me when we were kids,
"In every language
my name means 'illusion.'"

Who said, one summer, years later,
"I've been shy, uneasy.
You wouldn't know me."

Walking to her house
in the half-dark,
the honeysuckle makes me dizzy—

every one of me
she wouldn't know,
or I—everything I carry

absently with me
in my name,
"Matthew," from the Hebrew,

"gift of god."

Under every idea of the world,
the world itself,
holding at once every doubt and flower,

every illusion of itself,
joyful, difficult.

It deepens.
Doesn't strive.

Every one of her, of me.

for Maya Katz

At Family Parties, My Mother is Endlessly Social

She wants to seem unbelievably light—
wherever joy comes from, she wants to say she
can let it come, and forget about perfecting her life.

The fact that we're all together can forgive her intrusions,
make them casual half-jokes: her younger sister's
terrible ex-husband, the stink of her cigarettes, her boyfriend

who decided, again, not to be there, or her brother's
obsession with work, his crude humor.
When we eat, and any of the kids eat too fast,

she tells us how her father made her count
ten seconds between bites. It says a lot about you,
how you eat, she says. She laughs

when she says I could probably eat anything.
Whenever I'm quiet for too long, she starts to worry, but she tries
not to, stops herself sometimes from having to rescue me,

having to presume some fear of mine, and name it. Afterwards, she says
she thought I'd learned to talk better at parties, in large groups.
I ask her if I can just be quiet without her worrying, and she asks,

when do you think I worry? Doesn't she remember the party
when she mentioned to ten people that after twenty-five, the body stops
producing new bone, and everyone should really eat more calcium?

But that's the way the body is, she says, and she can't stop it.
She means it's dangerous, and she's right, most of the time,
about her life, the way she sees it. (The doctor says her bones are weak.)

She loves what she thinks she can't change because she loves
trying to change it, or to put it in a place where she can.
But I love Bob and Sue, she says, and we're just joking.

Joking around about that is fake to me, I say.
We're both stubborn, and secretly counting the seconds
until we can attend to some plain thing that makes

time pass, before starting to talk, as if we hadn't been.

Reminders to a Friend, to Myself

1.
The personality test
said you would've made an excellent detective

if you hadn't made up stories
inside the simulated crime scenes—

an animal skulking in the stairwell
with a clue, a scroll with the errand

you'll rush for, the wrong turn
that knows more about the story than you do—

in any new desire,
the danger of familiar need.

2.
The ogre buries fear
so far inside your body
that you need to unearth it

from his underground house.
The walls stink
from the effort of his sneer,

your dearest effort shed,

not in the body anymore
but *for* it, not in fear anymore
but *for* it. Desire for desire,

creature for creature,

put your ear to the ground, the tree, the air,
to what you were convinced you couldn't hear,
and listen—

Lightness

I hadn't noticed the cricket
until everything was quiet.

It became a massive note
I could never find,
and carried me.

Clouds loom like statues.
The unprepared roads will flood.

In from the garden, I let the ants
scurry over my legs and arms.

Photograph, for a Class on Perspective

She wanted to capture restlessness, I think,
or the way you're drawn to what's moving
if you stay impossibly still.

She nudged our heads to the left, to the right,
tried to get us to gaze at each other,
or at the candle she put there, between us.

When we moved or were too rigid for too long,
the three of us couldn't help laughing.
We thought: friends don't do this.

It was funny, how deception was there, and truth,
looking like some storybook romance,

like we were waiting for something—
sympathy, pity, self-pity.

We thought: friends don't let you see
that bare expectation, or how their bodies

shift when they fear they can't hide it
and you can't tell if they're watching or not watching

you or the light caught moving in your eyes.

Dead Bird

You drank death down,
or death drank you,

drew you in, your soul
fled, and blood
leaks from your bones now

into the street that offered itself,
that grew around you,
lit with you,

and every day, you were brought to me,
or I was brought to you
and your body's angles

pointing strictly back at themselves.

Flood

Driving through a flood with you,
trying to find my canes,
the tires don't touch the road.

My father's dying is the place we float in,
and I'm not quite moving
with grief, but stepping

into it, dragging my legs through,
but if I listen for breath,
it doesn't end,

and if I listen for your heart
in my heart, I can hold that continuance

closer to me than I can hold
my body to myself, and we're both

infinitely small, infinitely large.
I'm trying terribly to walk
through what holds me completely.

I should be swimming.
What are my feet?
Where is my name?

Suspicions

That the dream classroom
is a real classroom.

That I want the same frustration,
that cold, cramped seat, the same
chemistry formulas or history

I haven't studied because I haven't learned
not to want, or that wanting is a path

or nothing. That I call it something and want it
to stay so I can learn it in the good teacher's
lecture, the crux, the trick, the turn, the stop.

But I'm here and there is no teacher or
everything teaches, the desks, the paper, the margins, the wall,

and someone I love knocks on the wall
from the next room. The blackboard
shakes with it and spells it out in a cloud of chalk,

and I scribble to get right my tremor,
erase and revise confusion,
correct love to make it continuous.

But love is here, learning with me
every sequence and completion
to abandon. We bend over our desks and begin

frustration's undistracted gift.
Love is not attachment.
It's love's confusion I borrow and want.

Flowers

Back in the smaller house,
we call it "the old new house,"
as if it were waiting for us.

We take months to empty old boxes
and settle back in.
Wanting to make it more new,

my mother tapes a stencil near the ceiling
on the kitchen wall,

leans any place she can for balance,
cranes her neck awkwardly up
and paints them slowly—

purple flowers,
small petals
floating over separate stems.

This is the purple crayon flower
in one fluid line
on my friend's old letter,

the wide flower on my wall
that says "I finally learned
how to forgive myself,"

my mother straining to paint
where she, where we,
can't quite see.

Nesting Dolls

Split and mend, they say to their one body,
split and mend, as if the chest
had to open and open again

so the bodies inside it could wander.
But what about their immovable smile?
You have to twist them open to understand.

They still hear every skin shiver.
They've always just startled awake
with fastened buttons, braided hair.

Blizzard

We fold paper snowflakes.

I show my sister how to crease the edges
neatly with her nail, how
any shape you cut
replicates where it folds, and you can't know how
the whole thing looks until you tease it open.

We sweep tiny shapes from the floor,
missing the actual snow,
the ice that makes the daylight brighter.

Our father wants a picture.
Frozen branches, covered roads.

Hannah listens for where the snow goes when it melts.
She folds a swan to glide in the lake of her hand.

My Grandparents' Grief

They called my father by his dead brother's name.

They could hear Frankie breathing in their cabinets,
with the five-year-old unopened soda cans,
behind the butterfly wallpaper.

Grandma forgot her words, and Frankie swirled in the dust
of her dictionary, shook its rickety table.
He stirred the leaves of the spider plants she kept

in the severed bottom halves of milk jugs.
The leaves grew until they almost touched
the pictures of our half-forgotten relatives.

When Frankie killed himself, they couldn't love him
without an enduring refusal to forgive him.
They never said so, but I had my father's hair, his eyes, his voice,

so sometimes they'd call me without thinking—*Frankie,
Frankie*—and I'd correct them, and they'd mutter apologies.
Then Marty died, and Rose died two weeks later—

anger at him leaving had to consume her, too,
consume the years when Frankie was their name
for me, my father, or any of the family's particular grief.

Both of them dead, we called them Grandma, Grandpa, Dad, Ma.

Departure

Joints of the train shake,
racing to another country,
another life, leaving us—

the ghost of the world's pull.
I don't want you to be late.
I won't be, I won't be.

I'm not leaving,
but we still pull ourselves
through urgency,

insistence and sustenance
next to each other.

Leaving myself,
I want a witness
and have one,

in you and me, chopping food,
stirring pots on the stove,
stirring the train's clamor.

Hunger is not the word for hunger.
Tonight, we'll eat vegetables, potatoes,
and the steam still hugging the walls.

Design

Among the gate's foliage
one leaf is carved
upside-down, as if a hand slipped—

perhaps inevitably,
perhaps offered in compassion to a god
angered by perfection,

or offered as fear offers a place
to practice distraction
until it's deliberate, the lack

unfixed, the forest
overturned in its faithful mirror.

A Thought

1.
The purest kindness is undriven.

Any flicker of expectation
can trap me in its ocean-wave of want,
gather the world around me

like a storm, clawing,
tethered to the expected world,
deprived of a past. The smallest

disturbance a world of disturbance, the only
certainty. Duration feeds and worries me.

2.
Kindness says leave that place,
walk its edge with me,

away from the ambition
in every expected kindness,

trying to stop thought with thought,
covering your heart with your heart.

The ocean is rushing back to burn you with cold.
Escape the sameness of escape.

3.
Water's cloudy grit, and the pause
just before its wished-for fall—

turning away, I hold both worlds
as their orbits tumble

and the ground slips out,
bright with allowance and power.

Blessings

At the surprise party, we all sat clapping dumbly
when you came in unsurprised.

I fumbled in a cabinet, your voice
in the other room saying
I know we are of the same nature.

Three birds with clipped wings
try to glide up the dizzy staircase.
Claws rattle the banister.

Downstairs, a blackbird
rips the basement insulation.

I didn't know that was you
rustling in the upstairs window.
You didn't know I was listening—

dissembler, aberration, wellspring,
laughing with me in the luminous room,
where I'll say your name and you'll find me unsurprised.

Climbing

Sometimes you walk with such restless joy,
I wonder what you look like asleep.

In our long strides up to the trail,
all we've never said or gotten done
in sleep, in the spaces where we live.

This is where you held an old girlfriend.
These signs tell us the names of birds.

Over the sheer cliff,
from the closest we're allowed to look,
we can't see the edge of the ocean,

and I joke that it scares me, that we
could be higher than we think.

Our breaths hover over us
in the colder air,

and we're quieter now,
tired and silly from climbing.

Again, we've stayed too late.
This is the third Wednesday we can't go dancing.

No matter.
We feel by breathing.
We hear with our steps.

for Tessa Andermann

The Sky Inside the Shaking Tree

What came
before my hand
to make my hand?
If I squint
hard enough can I see
through it to the
things it's made of?
When was it
just a thought?
If I could look
up from the smallest
place inside it,
I'd see the huge
empty spaces
spinning in the atoms,
through the muscles
to the lines for my heart,
my fate, my mind, my life.

My fingers got blurry.
What if this (sitting
in the backseat
by myself) what if
this is a dream, the window
and my breath—bloom
fade, bloom?

My parents called me out
and I forgot
what it was I suddenly
knew. I knew it would
be there for me
some later time.

Meeting-place,
holding-place,
wayward angel, car window.

Both of us young, my father
swung me, when I cried, to a song

called "Communication Breakdown,"
the singer screaming

misunderstanding, screaming
the crescendo of
sweet, consolable grief.

Years later, no words, so we screamed
and muddied them, a first
departure from trust,

one staccato beat, one
high note searing through the body,

abandonment
played again and again to get at the words,
anger stirring in the lost thing.

But nothing is ever lost.
Love has in it no starting or ending point.

Anger at that continuance
kept us here
after all our broken-down words.

Body said

the dream of the world
is the fullness it holds
within itself.

What you feel
reveals you.

Watch
for the sustenance
inclined to a source,

enamored of singularity,
quickly here and quickly

gone, shadow from which
the body's courage comes.

Fireflies
apparently stumbling.

I slapped one on my leg.
Its blood glowed.

Sometimes, pain's exactitude
was how I moved. I slipped
into my exiles, my hesitations,
forest of my surest burdens,

and followed these down to where
I thought the thoughts were me
and held them still so I could catch
their edges and rake them out.

Every overstepping was one thing
then one thing then one thing then
another. Sometimes, I found myself
in this cruelty, tripping on the roots,

no familiar grief to extrapolate
and break. I rolled the body-stone
until it hurt, until these interruptions
dug a cradle in the earth to hold me,

body-cradle, my broken
bearing across, my one
undone thing wanting
not to stir. But there is no prelude

or conclusion to any known thing
here. In this bare field
there is a tree full of windy leaves.
I'm in the car with the broken radio

twitching the dial. Clouds churn
and swirl. I'm locked inside the static,
the field, the muscled roots,
the shaking tree and the sky waiting to rain. . . .

Loud breath
just before you couldn't breathe—

I want to go
back to the beach
but you can never really
own the beach.

You wanted to own
the sound of the ocean, its reach
swallowed inside you,
the wet sand, the children
digging moats around their castles.

What you wanted, you had.
A hem to pull and hold
in your thick blanket.

The holding
onto the thing *is* the thing.

It saves you once and slips,
continuous, into
its own vast music.

What you own, you own
in this relinquishing.

Dear heart, we will say
what needs to be said

but first I have to learn to breathe
deep enough to let it out.

You wouldn't let your eyes close
until we left the room.

You didn't want us to see
the life you grew closer to
in your sleep, that dreaming,

dreamt-of completion,
that clenched fist

inside you
growing faster than the rest of you.

I have to keep time for
what you couldn't wake from,

the same strict vowel
stuck in the throat.

You died with your mouth open, saying "I."

In the growing dark
you tried to get the lens still,
anxious for the point where light
could trick the scene into edges.

You got shadow and brightness
that fattened and swallowed
buildings and trees and waves.
You got black water and a blinding sky.

Mostly, the whale's tailfin disappeared
in the shivering sun,
but you got it perfect once,
almost falling over the boat's edge,

and I wonder if you still shift and squint
or if you're hidden inside that elegant fin
curling back towards the body you can't see.

The light is everywhere and nowhere.
The light that meets the sea *is* the sea.

A coyote
turned the corner with
perfect balance,

muscle shimmer
without a source—

being a source,
it turned as I turned,

circle I followed and followed,
body's fondest mystery—

turned elsewhere,
holding

in its bright stride
each
pained, exacting place.

You're swallowing
mouthfuls of the room

and I can't pour
water fast enough

past the edge of the glass
into you. I'm weighing

my body against this
unfamiliar air,

tipsy on the scale's chains,
the weighing-tray,
trying to hold still.

Your body can hold no prelude
to the world, to that music you are losing.

Devoured gatherer, devouring.

The promise of loss
is not the persistence I want.

Body under all of hunger's clothes.

Remembering is blood
and the dream of blood,

embodied, abundant,
cupped and suffered,

a failed source to feast on.
From the taken-in world came

one breath
full of outsideness

and nothing in it could feed me,
nothing in the thread the body follows

out, out, out, out, out.

Then, my skin,
and the lightness of waking up
from the years inside me.

Nothing of mine was there.
My anger's first refusal
is flying from my hands—

this is my laughter, my food,
this is the bird
cradled in the hands I love.

Holding its wings, not myself,
not anything I knew—
temple I never got to.

Dearest thief, I woke up
joking and still hungry
for the air under your wings,

that undivided, once-forsaken, saving thing.

The stillness I came to find, I found.
Two immensities
against each other,

one streak of light
reaching for the earth that waited there,

enough space for all my books and receipts
to fly from their boxes
into my other lives,

enough space to say
I didn't put this here but someone else,
these clouds, this storm, this wind,

someone else gathered what I needed
from what I kept,
and I was good.

I waited for that person.

From the grip of my patience,
the broken expectation is generous,
the loved thing

parts the air, anywhere.

This is light
breaking a sacred cup
on a stone floor.

Scar
down the center of my chest,
wanting to open

a hollow in the skin for singing.
Skin wants an inside
place to cry out from.

Hear the blood hum,
palimpsest. Breath
wants the hollow of the skin

to rest in, to flower.
Here, finally, enough
open space to hear in the

elsewhere-singing heart the drum of your one
voice calling out,
dear heart, from the inside.

My scar is falling upward
into the shape of the healing place.

The breath's
furthest edge finds its wheel,
keeps its turning.

Let what is given
return until nothing is ever left out.

Rabbit's eye
sets off running,

never stops—
thread the body follows

back to its fullness,
no holding-place,
no secrets

in those watchful eyes
here with me
wanting and ignoring nothing,

the quiet
of spirit or decision
deep inside

the sight that
becomes the body.

Our work is momentary and endless.

The whole landscape flickered
at once and was changed.

Even my patience,
every corner keeping

time inside it was
taken from me.

Do you understand?
I had one moment of being no one,

and there was enough space
to let each loved and hungered thing

have its relinquishing.
There was nothing

I could think to see outside of,
nothing to get or let go of,

no one change
trapped in itself, or in me.

This was the surrender I carried.
Under the loud world

another city, another sky,
and each of my lives

shifting with this brightness
inextricably, leading me

back to my timeless, real life.

Garden of dirty stones.
Sky the color of smoke.
Air so still

I have to move
to know it's there.

I drag my fingers through,
and roll one stone
until it's weightless

and the edges I hold and stand in

blur.
The first gift
of my blurring steps

is the space, the heat
I lean against.

I have to build a house for breath
from a sky the color of smoke.

Somewhere, a prayer book is burning,
and I have to move.
I have to watch.

Let the loud rain slip
into your collarbone,
down your chest,

past your legs, your feet.
From the green flurry of names
bring your hands together.

Here, one world leaks into another.
Begin with a stone. Skim it
quickly with the wrist,

let it go at the right moment and it
leaps from its meeting-place,
your face and the whole craved landscape

shaking. Search out
the furthest edge, bear it
through the roots, the leaves, the water

seeking the lowest place,
this gratefulness shaking
free from our throats,

finally. Let the muddy edges
assemble, earth-cradle, fissure
and root. Bring your hands

together in greeting or prayer.
This is the cup I stumbled with,
careless, so full of care.

Dear heart, gather the mirrored shards.
Take the most exposed place, console it.
Whisper blessings for the hands.